76 Excel Tips
to Increase Your Productivity and Efficiency

Nick Weisenberger

Copyright Information

First Edition – Paperback version
Copyright ©2014 by Nick Weisenberger
ISBN-13: 978-1499100853
ISBN-10: 149910085X

Table of Contents

Chapter 1: Introduction

The Author's Story

I wrote this guide because when I was in a time of desperate need, not too long ago, becoming super proficient with Microsoft Excel helped advance my professional career. I was working as a new mechanical engineer at a struggling company where everyone else was much more experienced than I was. I realized that made me expendable. When the economy took a turn for the worse, and coworkers began getting laid off, I feared for my job and my family's future. I needed a way to set myself apart to prove my value to the team. Learning how to write VBA macros in Excel gave me a huge advantage over my coworkers. Additionally, once I was able to create Excel macros I was able to apply that knowledge to other software, such as CAD systems, which helped to quickly earn my colleague's respect, leading not only to me keeping the job but also to quicker promotions, along with more job freedom and flexibility. Not only did it help me bounce back from a low point but it opened my eyes to the world of productivity, efficiency, and automation and the opportunities that it can create for anyone's career. And if I can do it then you can too!

76 Excel Tips to Increase Your Productivity and Efficiency is my way of giving back for all of the fortunate things that have happened to me ever since. This is a guide, and the purpose of this guide is to do just that – guide you. If I can help just one person learn one thing that will help them in their career and/or life, all the time and effort I have put into writing these Excel tips will have been totally worth it!

Why use Excel?

Why use Microsoft Excel? With its wide variety of extreme uses, Microsoft Excel is the Swiss Army Knife of software tools. From a hand-made quilt designer to a 3D graphics engine, Excel is one of the most versatile and user friendly programs around. It doesn't matter what your skill level is - anyone can learn to use Excel!

Millions of people use Excel spreadsheets everyday but a vast majority of them have not unlocked the full potential of this incredible program. In fact, it's said 80% of the users only use 20% of the features. The purpose if this text is to increase your knowledge in order to improve your productivity and efficiency. If you've ever thought to yourself "there has to be a better way to do this," you're probably right and this book is for you.

Expectations

This book is not a beginner's guide nor is it for those who have never used Excel before. A basic understanding of the software is required. The purpose is to share tips and tricks you can put to use and get results immediately. The text was written primarily for Microsoft Excel 2013 for Windows. Most tips should work for all versions but please be aware some may not. All the tips have been grouped into different categories but besides that are not listed in any particular order. The table of contents can be used as a quick index and there is a list of resources in the Appendix located at the back of the book.

Chapter 2: Excel Shortcuts

Learning to use keyboard shortcuts is one of the best ways to increase your productivity with Microsoft Excel. Excel is a powerful tool, but you can't call yourself a power user until you've mastered the essential keyboard shortcuts. I've mostly avoided the obvious and essential shortcuts that also work in other apps (such as Ctrl+Z for undo and Ctrl+C for copy, Ctrl+B for bold, etc.) but besides those here are the Excel shortcuts you need to know:

Tip 1: Access the Excel help file – F1

Press F1 to access the Excel help file. Excel has hundreds of keyboard shortcuts so one of the most useful features of the help file is to search for 'keyboard shortcuts.' You'll find the full list of shortcuts there but the ones listed here are the most popular shortcuts you'll keep returning to.

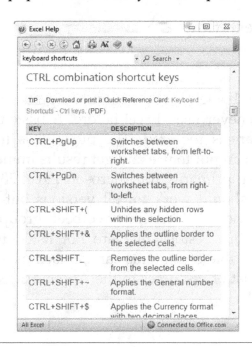

Tip 2: Show or hide formulas – CRTL+`

Not sure which formulas are running in your spreadsheet? Use Ctrl+` (the accent key, to the left of the number 1 key) to see the formulas in the cells rather than their results.

Tip 3: Access the ribbon – Alt

Every single Ribbon command in Excel can be accessed via the keyboard. Hit Alt and you'll see a letter (or a two-letter combination) above each ribbon tab. Type that letter or combo to use it. I've added the camera to the ribbon to quickly take screenshots, using Alt+4, as shown below.

Tip 4: Enter the current date – Crtl+;

Using Ctrl+; saves time checking and entering the date. Please note this is a fixed date and not the =TODAY() function.

Tip 5: Navigate between worksheets – Crtl+PgUp/PgDn

Complex Excel spreadsheets often have multiple worksheets. Rather than clicking on the bottom-of-screen tabs, use Ctrl+PgUp and Ctrl+PgDn to quickly navigate between sheets. Every second of time saved adds up.

Tip 6: Select an entire row or column – Ctrl/Shift+Space

For even more selection power, Ctrl+Space selects an entire column while Shift+Space selects an entire row. You can then use the shift keys plus the arrow keys as appropriate to select additional rows or columns. Remember, *C=Column=Crtl.*

Tip 7: Sum function – Alt+=

Here is the fastest way to sum your data in Excel: after entering your data in the column, click the first empty cell in that column and enter ALT+= (equals key), then click Enter. It will add up the numbers in all the cells above it.

Tip 8: Jump to top or bottom – Crtl+Up/Down

This tip is particularly useful when you're dealing with large number of rows. Use this method instead of endless scrolling to save time. Enter CTRL + ↑ (upward arrow key) to jump to the top cell or CTRL +↓(downward arrow key) to jump to the last cell before an empty cell.

Tip 9: Multiple lines in one cell (line break) – Alt+Enter

In some cases you may want multiple lines of data or text you typed into a cell to appear on several lines (also called inserting a line break). Instead of entering the text in another cell, press ALT+ENTER. That way you'll start a new line while typing or editing data.

Tip 10: Hide columns or rows – Crtl+0/9

To quickly hide a row / rows use CTRL+9. To hide a column / columns use CTRL+0.

Tip 11: Switch between tools – F6

For all those anti-mouse users out there, F6 is the ultimate shortcut. It allows you to switch between the worksheet, the ribbon, task pane, and zoom controls. The less mouse movements you have to do, the more time you can save.

Tip 12: Copy cell above selected - Crtl+'

If you type Ctrl+' it looks at the cell above the selected cell and copies it into the current cell.

Tip 13: Cancel changes - Esc

Press ESC while you are editing the text or formula in a cell to exit the cell and cancel any changes that you may have made.

Tip 14: List of functions – Shift+F3

Not sure if you need to use a SUMIF or COUNTIF? You know there's probably a function for what you need to do but can't remember the name? Open the list of available functions using Shift+F3.

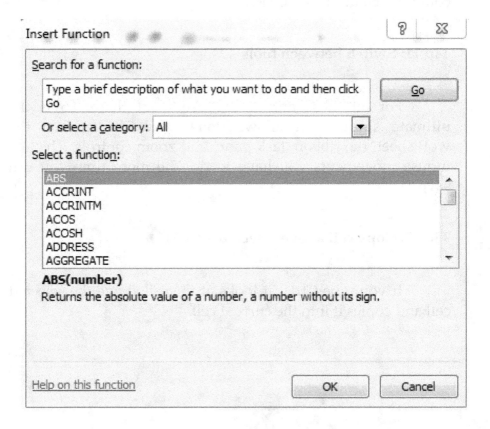

Tip 15: Create bookmarks and other – Crtl+g

Use Ctrl+g > Special to do things like select all cells with comments, select all cells containing formulas, etc. You can also create a bookmark within a large spreadsheet by naming a cell. Then use CTRL+g to quickly navigate to that cell (for example, create a "HOME" cell).

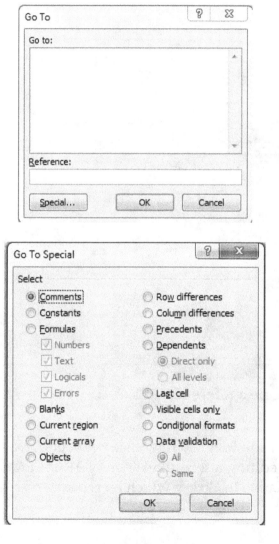

Tip 16: Format cells – Crtl +1

Do you constantly find yourself formatting a cell by changing the font border and fill? Use CRTl+1 to display the Format Cells dialog box. Eliminate as many mouse clicks as possible!

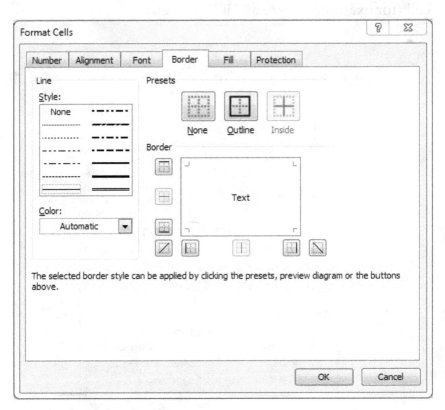

Tip 17: Toggle a reference – F4

Use F4 to toggle a reference between A1, $A$1, A$1 and $A1 while editing a formula When NOT editing a formula, F4 is an alternative to Ctrl+y which is "repeat" or "redo".

Tip 18: Update formulas - CRTL+ALT+SHIFT+F9

CTRL+ALT+SHIFT+F9 rechecks dependent formulas, and then calculates all cells in all open workbooks, including cells not marked as needing to be calculated. Very useful when you have user defined functions.

Tip 19: Change date to number format - CTRL+SHIFT+~

When Excel automatically formats a number as a date, you can change it back to a number using the shortcut CTRL+SHIFT+"~" (or change the date format using CRTL+SHIFT+#).

Tip 20: Launch the macro editor - Alt + F11

One of my personal favorite and most used Excel shortcuts is ALT+F11 to open the macro editor. Some of my most used macros are how to create folders from Excel and combine multiple Excel files, listed in a later chapter in this book.

Tip 21: Insert the degree symbol – Alt+0176

Use the shortcut Alt + 0176 to insert a degree symbol (°). As with most software these days, there are a number of different ways to get to the same result. You can also use character map to use the symbol you are looking for. A character map of all special symbols, including foreign language characters, can be displayed by typing "charmap" into the Search window at the bottom of the Start Menu (in Windows). Choose the font corresponding to the one you're using and click on a character. Next click Select>Copy to copy the character. Return to your document, click where you want the character inserted, and go to Edit>Paste (or do Ctrl+V) to insert it. Finally, the simplest way is simply to where MSOffice users can go to Insert>Symbol to accomplish the exact same thing.

Tip 22: Quickly correct data in multiple cells – Crtl+Enter

If you want to quickly correct data in multiple cells, follow these simple steps: select all of the cells containing the data you want to replace. If those cells are non-adjacent, highlight them by holding down CTRL and clicking to select each cell. Now, type the correct data, press CTRL+ENTER and watch the newly entered data appear in all of the selected cells. The other way to do this is by using "Find and replace" tool. You can access it by entering CTRL+H.

Chapter 3: Improve Your Formatting and Viewing

Tip 23: Quickly apply the same formatting to different cells

There is a quick and non-manual way of applying the same formatting to different cells. Simply apply desired formatting options to one cell, select it and double-click the "Format Painter" button (you can find it in "Home"tab -> "Clipboard group"). The formatting options you chose are now locked, and you can apply them to any other cell by clicking each cell you want to format. To turn the lock off, double-click the "Format Painter" button.

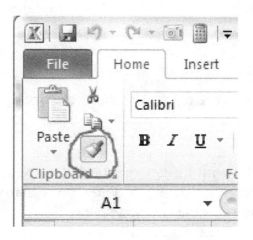

Tip 24: Create a template

To avoid entering the same formatting options for every new spreadsheet, you can create a template with commonly used formatting options which will serve as a model for other spreadsheets. After entering the necessary data, creating formulas, charts and other stuff you need, apply the desired formatting options. Then click on the Office button (round button with MS Office 2007 logo in the top left corner). When the drop-down menu opens, choose these options: "Save as" -> "Other formats" -> "Save as" -> "Save as type". For saving, you can choose from three types of templates depending on your needs:

➢ Excel Macro Enabled Template (*.xltm), if your template contains macros;
➢ Excel 97-2003 Template (*.xlt), if you plan to use your template with older versions of Excel;
➢ Excel Template (*.xltx), for all other templates.

Once saved, your template can be accessed by clicking the Office button -> "New"-> "My templates"–> *select your template* -> "Ok".

Tip 25: Change the default number of sheets

Every time you open a new workbook in Microsoft Excel it opens with three worksheets (by default). You can, of course, insert more sheets or delete ones that you don't need. The good news is the unused sheets don't occupy additional memory or increase your file size, but deleting or adding sheets is an additional, unnecessary step and eliminating can save you some time. In this case, you can actually change the default value of the number of sheets the Excel automatically opens with.

Excel 2003: Go to: TOOLS>OPTIONS and click General in the Options dialog box. Next, change the setting for "Sheets in new workbook".

Excel 2007: Select the office window button>Excel Options. On the popup menu you will see the section "when creating new workbooks." Change the "include this many sheets" from three to whatever you desire.

Now all new workbooks will have the number of sheets you specify. Because I usually find myself deleting the extra sheets I typically change this number to one unless I know I am going to have a monster spreadsheet.

Tip 26: Inspect your sheets easily by lining them in the same worksheet

There is an option in Excel that enables you to get two or more sheets from the same worksheet to appear on the same screen. Simply choose the "New Window"-> "View Side by Side" option on the "View" tab. The "Synchronous Scrolling"options for scrolling through both pages by dragging the slider bar in one of them is turned on by default. You can turn it off if you prefer to scroll through each of your sheets separately.

Tip 27: Two users, one workbook

Did you know you can have more than one user edit an Excel spreadsheet at the same time? In Excel 2007 and newer, simply go to the Review tab and click "**Share Workbook**" (to the right of Protect Workbook). Next, click the box labeled "Allow changes by more than one user at the same time." That's it!

In the pop-up window below this label it will show you who currently has the spreadsheet open. There's also an advanced tab for you to setup other options like tracking history, automatic save times, and how to handle conflicting changes between users. Finally, you can use Track Changes to see who made what changes at what time.

Of course, enabling Share Workbook only allows you to share the workbook with multiple users over a local network. To allow sharing over the internet (similar to Google Docs) use the **Excel Web App** by going to: **File > Save & Send > Save to Web** (Excel 2010 and newer only, must have a Windows Live account). This has become a very useful feature at my day job by eliminating multiple copies of the same spreadsheets.

Tip 28: Customize the Quick Access Toolbar

One of the best shortcut features of Excel may be one of the least used: customizing the quick access toolbar. For example, the option of using a calculator for simple calculations while working in Excel can be convenient from time to time. Newer versions of Excel have a calculator feature, but it is hidden by default. To get the calculator on your Excel screen, go to Excel options > Customize. Or click the "Customize Quick Access Toolbar" button (the down arrow symbol next to the "Redo" button on the top left of the screen) and then click "More Commands." In an opened "Options" dialog under "Choose commands" select "All commands." Scroll down to find the "Calculator" command, click "Add" -> "Ok". The "Calculator" button is now placed in "Quick Access" toolbar and ready to use.

Another great use of the quick access toolbar is adding the camera command. If you're constantly taking screen captures of your spreadsheets for presentations or emails you can do it directly from Excel by using the camera feature. Click the camera feature then highlight the area you want to take a screenshot of. It creates an image directly in your spreadsheet that you can then copy and paste into another document.

Tip 29: Modify the ENTER key behavior

You can change the default ENTER key behavior from dropping down to the cell below to anything else to better suite your needs (moving to the cell to right, left or up). Go to "File" tab, select "Options"->"Advanced" and select your desired option from the first drop-down menu under the "Editing options".

Tip 30: Quickly adjust the width of one or multiple columns

You can improve neatness of your spreadsheet by adjusting a column (or more of them) to the width of its content. It is easily done by clicking on the header of the column you want to adjust, moving your cursor to the right side of the header and double-clicking it when it turns into a plus sign. To adjust width of more than one column, select them with CTRL-clicking and repeat the steps described above.

Tip 31: Insert or delete multiple rows or columns

This Excel feature might be especially useful when you want to add or delete lots of data from the middle of a worksheet. When adding more rows, first select the data you want your additional rows to be inserted within, then right-click, click "Insert" and choose "Shift cells down" option. If you want to delete data, repeat the process with selecting "Delete" instead of "Insert" and "Shift cells up" instead of "Shift cells down". If you want to insert entire row or column across your whole worksheet (not just selected table of data), select the option "Entire row" or "Entire column" after right-clicking on the area you highlighted.

Tip 32: Automatically fill a series of cells with sequential pattern

If you want to fill a selected row or column with consecutive numbers there is no need for creating a formula to fill a series or for doing it manually. Instead, type your first value, place the cursor at the bottom right corner of the cell and drag it in the direction you want the series filled. Then, click the "Auto fill options" handle that appeared next to the cursor and select the "Fill Series" option in the drop-down menu. In case your data increases or decreases with a different pattern (not by 1), you'll need to enter two or three values in the cells manually before selecting all of them and repeating the process described above. That will enable Excel to recognize your data pattern and fill the rest for you.

Tip 33: Create custom auto fills

Creating auto fills to complete columns or rows of sequential data can be a real time-saver. To add your own custom lists, click the "Office" button, select "Excel Options"->"Popular"->"Edit Custom Lists"->"New List". Then click in the "List Entries" column, type each of your entries in the list, followed by ENTER and confirm everything by clicking "Add".

Tip 34: Quickly select all the blank cells

Sometimes you may want to select just the blank cells in the range of cells you have, e.g. for entering a value or formula into only the blank cells. Here is the quick way to do it without manually clicking on every one. Select the range of cells from which you want to select only the blank cells. Then, press F5 on your keyboard, click the "Special..." button, select the option "Blanks" and click "OK". You will notice that only the blank cells in the range have been selected.

Tip 35: Remove duplicate entries

To remove duplicate entries go to the Data tab, click Remove Duplicates, then click Select All or pick which columns to remove duplicates. Click OK. A window will pop up letting you know how many duplicates were removed, if any, and how many unique values remain.

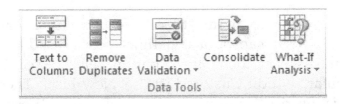

Tip 36: Highlight duplicate cells

To highlight duplicate cells without deleting them, first select the cells where you want to find the duplicate values. Next, in the Styles area of the Home tab, select Conditional Formatting, then choose Highlight Cells Rules --> Duplicate values.

Tip 37: Custom sort / Sort by color

If you're like me, you like to color your Excel cells depending on any number of factors: priority (red, yellow, and green), whether a value is up or down (green and red), or just to highlight it to draw your attention to it the next time you open the workbook (any color you like!). To do this, simply click the Text Highlight button on the ribbon and select your color. Once your color is chosen, simply select any additional cells you want to mark and click the button again.

That's all very handy, but did you know that you can sort by the color of your cells? Select the cells you wish to sort. On the ribbon under Sort & Filter, select Custom Sort. Now select the column you want to sort, select Cell Color under Sort On and then any color choices you have made will appear in the Order dropdown. This works just as well for Font Color. So now all of that cell and font coloring you've done can be really useful.

Tip 38: Use the context menus

A context menu is a menu that appears after a user interaction, such as a right mouse click. If you right click the worksheet tab scrolling buttons (the little black arrows to the left of the sheet tabs), you get a context menu listing all the sheets in the spreadsheet so you can jump to the sheet you want (useful when you have more sheets than you can see at one time).

Tip 39: How to hide individual numbers in Excel

If you highlight an area and go into the Custom formatting category of the Number formatting, entering the code ;;; makes any entries in that area invisible but still available to be used in calculations -- handy when you can't hide an entire column for whatever reason.

Tip 40: Filtering

Learning how to filter in Excel will help you analyze data faster and become better at your job. Filtering in Excel enables you to display only the data that you want to see on your spreadsheet without deleting anything. It's a really great way to search through large amounts of information.

There are three types of filters in Excel: list of values, by format, or criteria and you can sort your spreadsheet by order, color or text. What's the difference between sorting and filtering? Sorting will rearrange the order of your list while filtering keeps the order but actually hides data based on your filter criteria. To add a Filter in Excel, you can first select a single cell within your range of data but I recommend you highlight all your data (please note you cannot add filters to empty cells). Next, go to the Home tab then the Editing section. Under Sort & Filter click Filter (or use the filter shortcut *Crtl+Shift+L*). Once filtering is turned on you will see little arrows along your top row of data. Select one of the arrows to set your filter options. If you hover your mouse over the drop down arrow you will see a pop-up message displaying what the value the filter is currently set to (example: equals "Test").

To remove the filtering from your spreadsheet, simply click the Filter button again. If you want to reset the filter to the original values click on the Sort & Filter button and then click "Clear."

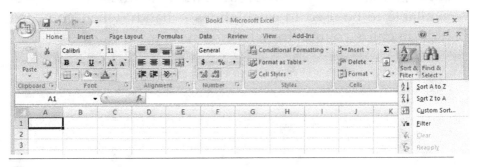

Tip 41: Create collapsible rows or groups

One method often used to collapse rows or columns in Excel is by using the Group function. Go to the Data tab, select the rows or columns you want to group, then select the **Group** icon (located in the Outline are). This will result in a button being placed to the left of the row number column and allow you to instantly collapse or hide the grouped rows. To ungroup the rows simply hit the **Ungroup** button (also in the Outline area).

You can use keyboard shortcuts to improve your speed and efficiency when applying this method. First, select the Row or Column range, then;

- ➤ To group: < Shift> <Alt> <RightArrow>
- ➤ To ungroup: < Shift> <Alt> <LeftArrow>
- ➤ To retain the Groups, but toggle hide/unhide the symbols: < Ctrl> <8>
- ➤ (Using the "8" that's under the function keys, *not* from the num keypad.)

Another option to group rows would be to apply **Subtotals** to your range. You'll get those outlining symbols and even a subtotal row between each group. The Subtotals button is also in the Outline section of the Data tab.

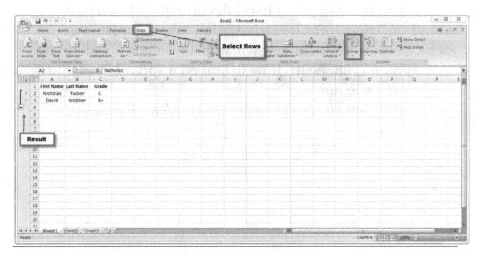

Tip 42: Use Microsoft's OneDrive cloud storage service

Save documents, spreadsheets, and presentations online, in OneDrive. Share them with others and work together at the same time. Get started now, it's free! To create an Office document using **Office Web Apps**, just go to the **OneDrive website**, tap or click **Create** on the bar at the top, and then choose the type of file you want to create. When you tap or click an Office document on the OneDrive website, it automatically opens in Office Web Apps. Office Web Apps preserve your document formatting, so you can make quick edits without worrying about messing up how the document looks.

When you use OneDrive, you can share documents with other people and all work on the same copy instead of sending different versions back and forth in email. Your classmates, friends, or coworkers can use free Office Web Apps to view or edit the documents, even if they don't have Office installed. With OneDrive, you can even work on documents with other people at the same time without creating conflicts. For more info about sharing files in OneDrive, see **Share files and folders and change permissions:** http://windows.microsoft.com/en-us/onedrive/share-file-folder.

You can embed an Excel document that you have stored on **Microsoft OneDrive**. After you complete these steps, your excel document will appear on your post or page — graphs and all. Learn how to embed a spreadsheet into a blog or website here:

http://en.support.wordpress.com/excel-web-app/

Chapter 4: Formulas & Functions

I highly recommend you become familiar with as many Excel functions as possible. All formulas in Excel begin with the equals (=) sign and are followed by a function's name (SUM, IF, COUNT, etc.). Functions are predefined formulas. For a list of available functions, click a cell and press **SHIFT+F3**. Arguments pertain to all the information required to evaluate a function (the IF function has three arguments). The spacing between arguments and the order of elements is also critical. All parentheses must be closed and many arguments require a comma in-between them. Apostrophes (') and hyphens (-) are ignored, with one exception: if two text strings are the same except for a hyphen, the text with the hyphen is sorted last.

Tip 43: Apply the same formula to multiple cells

Using this Excel tip will save you from retyping the same formula over and over again. Create the needed formula in the first cell. Place your cursor at the bottom right corner of the cell and double-click to copy your formula into the rest of the cells in that column. Each of those cells will then show the result of the applied formula using the data specific to each row.

Tip 44: Name a range of data for quicker access

It's easier to work with a range of data if it is specified by a name rather than by its cell addresses (which could change). That's why Excel has the option of giving a name to a range of data. It can be done by selecting a block of cells you want to name, clicking on "Formulas" tab ->"Define Name". Enter the name you want and an explanatory comment to remember the purpose of that range. Any spaces you include in the name will be converted automatically to an underscore character. Confirm by clicking "Ok". Afterwards, you can access that specific range of data anytime by clicking the drop-down list from the "Name" box at the left of the formula bar, and then clicking on its name.

Tip 45: Easiest way to see a sum or average of your data

If you only want to see a sum or average of your data without entering the result value in your worksheet, there is an easy way to do it. Simply type a few numbers in adjacent cells and highlight them – the average of numbers, their sum and the count of the cells will be displayed at the status bar at the bottom of the Excel window. This can also be done with non-adjacent cells: click on one cell, then click on the other cells containing numbers that you want to sum, while holding down the CTRL key all the time. The average and sum of numbers as well as count of the cells will show up at the status bar, updating each time you click another cell.

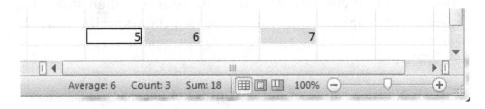

Tip 46: Shade alternate rows

Shading alternate rows improves legibility of lengthy lists that contain lots of data. Applying cell shading can be done simply by using Excel's Conditional Formatting. First, you need to highlight the range of cells, rows or columns you want to format. Then, choose Format->Conditional Formatting->New Rule->Use a formula to determine which cells to format. Now, enter "=MOD(ROW(),2)=0" into the "Format values where this formula is true" field. Click Format, select the Patterns tab and specify a color you want to shade your rows with. Confirm by clicking "Ok". It is recommended to choose light colors for shading to keep the default black text legible, unless you want to change the text color as well.

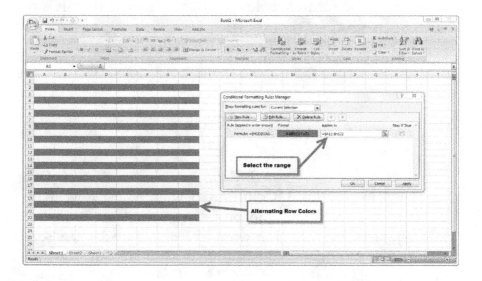

Tip 47: Avoid displaying errors

How do you avoid errors in Excel formulas? Sometimes, when you create a new formula you may get an error message in return (Here's a complete list of errors you may see in Excel: #N/A, #VALUE!, #REF!, #DIV/0!, #NUM!, #NAME?, #NULL!). In some cases, you'll want to know when a formula error occurs, but more often than not you would rather avoid these messages. You can do so by using an IF() function to check for an error. Use this standard format:

=IF(ISERROR(ORIGINALFORMULA),"",ORIGINALFORMULA)

For example, the formula below displays a blank if the division results in an error.

=IF(ISERROR(A1/B1),"",A1/B1)

Tip 48: Skip the weekends date formula

I have Date Started data in column A and Date Completed in column B. Column C I want to list how many days it took to complete the project so I subtract A from B (=B2-A2). However, I do not want to include weekends. So, if the start date is Friday and end date is Monday, currently my simple formula would display 4 days. I would like to create a formula that automatically skips over Saturday and Sundays, thus displaying the correct number of days as 2. How can this be accomplished?

Well, Excel actually has a built in function for this very

reason. It is called **NETWORKDAYS**. It returns the number of whole workdays between two dates. To accomplish my task I simply use this formula, starting in cell C2: **=NETWORKDAYS(A2,(B2-1))** Now you can calculate the number of work days there are between the start and end dates of a project by automatically excluding weekends.

Tip 49: Rank without ties

The RANK function returns the rank of a number in a list of numbers relative to the other values in that list. Here's the syntax:

=RANK(number, ref)

A potential problem is RANK will skip a number if there is a tie, so instead of getting a result of 1,2,3,4 you would get 1,2,2,4. To not skip any numbers with the RANK function use this alternative formula:

=RANK(num, ref) + COUNTIF(range,num)-1

See an example of how this formula is used here:

http://excelspreadsheetshelp.blogspot.com/2013/12/2013-college-bowl-pool-spreadsheet.html

Tip 50 and 51: LARGE Function and Arrays

I have a workbook with two worksheets. On Sheet1, in column A, there is a list of more than 2000 individual's names (some of them repeated) and column B lists each person's average test score percentage. In the second worksheet, called Sheet2, column A contains a list of each person's name exactly once and in columns b, c, d I want to list their first, second, and third best score or percentage.

The first, second, or third best score can be obtained using the Excel large function. The LARGE function allows you to return the nth largest value in a unique data set, like the second best score. The syntax is: **=LARGE(array,k)** where an **array** is a range of data and k is the position from the largest value in the array. So, for the first best score k=1, second best k=2, etc.

The LARGE function will get the best score from the list but we need to make it so the function only applies to the individual listed in sheet 2 column A. This is where the excel array function is used.

An array is a range of data, like items in a table. Often times you may see array formulas referred to as "CSE formulas," because you press CTRL+SHIFT+ENTER to transform the function into an excel array formula. We need to use our LARGE function in an array in order to return the best score based on the condition of the person's name.

To return the 2nd largest score for Joe, the name listed in Sheet2 column A, use this formula:

{=LARGE(IF(Sheet1!$A$1:$A$2000=$A2,Sheet1!$B$1:$B$2000,-1),2)}

Remember, to enter this array formula into the cell, then instead of hitting the Enter key, hit Ctrl-Shift-Enter.

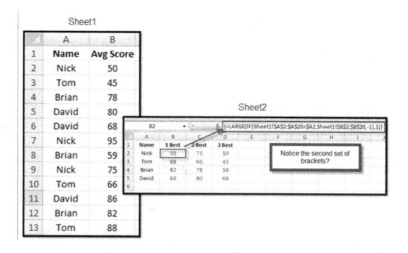

Tips 52: Named ranges

Use Named Ranges if you want your formulas to use natural language or variable names rather than cell references. So, instead of =A2*A4+B6 you could have =m*x+b.

Tip 53: Line Break

Enter a Line Break within a cell using a formula: ="abc"&CHAR(10)&"def" (then set the Wrap Text property).

Tip 54: Convert formulas to values

If you have a large block (say a column) of formulas you'd like to convert to values: Highlight the cells then right click on the BORDER and drag to the destination cell (without letting go of the mouse). Next, release the mouse button and a context menu will appear with "Copy Here as Values Only" option available.

Tip 55: Change the reference of formulas

If you have a group of formulas that you want to copy and change the references of, use the find and replace tool to replace all = with #. Copy and paste the cells, change what you need, then use find and replace again, this time replacing # with =.

Tip 56: Dynamic Lookup

One of my favorite Excel tips: **Dynamic Lookup** or Dynamic Searching by using a combination of VLOOKUP and MATCH functions. Basically, this function combo makes it so that the column that you pull the data from is dynamic based on the header making it more flexible than VLOOKUP by itself because you don't have to rely on knowing the index column number.

In this example, in cell B2 I have this formula that combines VLOOKUP and MATCH:

=VLOOKUP($A2, $D$2:$G$14,MATCH($B$1,$D$1:$G$1,0),FALSE)

| | B3 | | | ▾ | f_x | =VLOOKUP($A3, $D$2:$G$14, MATCH($B$1,$D$1:$G$1,0),FALSE) |

	A	B	C	D	E	F	G	H	I	J	K
1	Student	Scores		Student	Test1	Test2	Scores				
2	Nick	71		Tim	88	92	90				
3	Bowman	71.5		David	67	99	83				
4	Tim	90		Tyler	75	87	81				
5	Tyler	81		Bowman	77	66	71.5				
6	David	83		Nick	66	76	71				
7											
8											
9											
10											
11											
12											
13											
14											
15											
16											
17											

|◀ ◀ ▶ ▶| Dynmaic Lookup Example / Thank You / ⏺

The column header in B matches one of the column headers in D, E, F, G - it doesn't matter which one, you can change it and the values update automatically, which is the beauty of this formula. This makes it easy to add or remove columns without having to update your formulas. Not only is it more dynamic, the index column need not be on the left.

Chapter 5: Pictures, Charts, and Tables

Tip 57: Add a background image to your spreadsheet

Sometimes adding a background image can really spruce up the way your spreadsheet looks. You can do it easily by clicking the "Page Layout" tab, then the "Background" option in the "Page Setup" group. Now you can browse the image you want to set as background and double-click it to confirm your selection.

Tip 58: Align your charts

Dealing with two or more charts on a worksheet can make aligning them and matching their size a bit tricky. An easy way to get it done is by following these steps. Select the first chart by clicking on it. Then, hold down the CTRL key and click on every other chart you want to align with each other. When they are all selected, right-click on any one of them and choose "Size and properties". It will open the "Format Shape" dialog box, where you have to enter the measurements which will apply to all of the selected charts. When you have that confirmed with "Ok", go to the "Drawing Tools" tab and click "Format". By using the "Align" drop-down menu you can align your charts and distribute them evenly the way you want (horizontally or vertically).

Tip 59: Compress the graphical elements in your Excel spreadsheet

Pictures and other graphical elements embedded in your spreadsheet can greatly increase the document size, which makes the spreadsheet difficult to email or post online. The size of the document can be made smaller simply by compressing all the pictures in the spreadsheet. Select one of the pictures and notice the "Format" tab under "Picture Tools". Then, choose option "Compress Pictures" in the "Adjust" group, click "Options" and make sure that the options to delete cropped parts of the picture and to apply basic compression when saving are both enabled. Select the level of compression you want and confirm by clicking "Ok" twice.

Tip 60: Copy your chart or a set of cells to a different location as a picture

When you need to use your chart or a set of cells in software, consider copying it as a picture. That way all of your formatting options will be preserved. Although, be sure you did all your data processing before because you won't be able to do it afterwards.

To do this, select the chart or cell range you wish to copy. Click the downward arrow below "Paste"->"As Picture"->"Copy as Picture"->. Now you can paste the image to a new location outside Excel.

Tip 61: Types of charts

Generally, our ability to compare areas isn't as good as our ability to compare lengths, so you should use bar graphs instead of pie graphs whenever possible.

Tip 62: Pivot tables

Excel Pivot Tables help you take a table (or list) of data and instantly create a report from it. It's arguably the most powerful feature of Excel. Arrange your data in a table like fashion with no blank rows. Next, select your data (or any cell within the data) and go to Insert > PivotTable from the Ribbon (or press ALT+DP). In the Create PivotTable dialog box, make sure the range matches your data. You'll find that PivotTables have useful applications in many areas, including finance, sales, marketing, manufacturing, education, quality assurance, customer support, information technology, engineering, and more.

Tip 63: Count almost anything with a pivot table

You might think you have to be working with numbers to use a PivotTable, but by default, a PivotTable will count any text field. For example, suppose you have a list of employees and want to get a count by department. Just create a PivotTable normally, and then add Department as a Row Label, and the field First Name as a Value. Because First Name contains names as text the PivotTable will count entries in that field. As a bonus, this is a useful way to quickly get a list of every unique value that appears in a field. For example, this

PivotTable could show the departments that appear in a list of 300 or 30,000 employees.

To learn more about Pivot Tables read **Excel 2013 Pivot Table Data Crunching** by Bill Jelen (MrExcel) and Michael Alexander.

Chapter 6: VBA Macros

There are many Excel users who want to write macros but simply don't have time to sit down and learn everything they need to know. I will cover those core items to help teach beginners important concepts needed to create custom macros and will show experienced users additional tips and tricks.

What is a Macro and why do we use them? If you perform a task repeatedly, you can take advantage of a macro to automate the task. A macro is a series of functions, written in a scripting language, that you group in a single command to perform the requested task automatically. Macros use programming but you don't need to be a programmer or have programming knowledge to use them (though it definitely helps). Macros are used to save time and reduce the possibility of human error by automating repetitive processes, standardization, improving efficiency, expanding Excel's capabilities, and by streamlining tasks.

Macros are created by two primary methods:

1. Macro recorder
2. Write custom code with the macro editor

Record Macros is a good tool if you're stuck or unsure what syntax to use. You can record a few activities related to what you want to accomplish then look at the code that was created in the developer. However, record macros won't cover certain aspects of coding, particularly the control flow of the code. One won't see loops, if-else statements, or select case statements in recorded macros. One of the best ways to learn about macros is by looking at and using code that others have written and is proven to work

Tip 64: Email workbook

How often do you find yourself emailing a spreadsheet once you've completed it? Eliminate the extra step of opening email, attaching a documents, etc. by sending the spreadsheet directly from Excel via a macro. Here's an example:

```
Sub Email()
ActiveWorkbook.SendMail recipients:="---@---.com"
End Sub
```

Tip 65: Close all open workbooks macro

Sometimes you may want to close all files without saving. Doing it manually is a hassle with all the "Do you wanna save?" question pop ups. Here is a simple macro to close all files automatically:

```
Sub CloseAll()
Application.DisplayAlerts = False
myTotal = Workbooks.Count
For i = 1 To myTotal
   ActiveWorkbook.Close
Next i
End Sub
```

Tip 66: Turn on filter with a macro

Earlier I discussed the advantages of filtering. You can also turn auto-Filter on and off with a VBA macro. Here's how:

```
Sub TurnAutoFilterOn()
'check for filter, turn on if none exists
If Not ActiveSheet.AutoFilterMode Then
ActiveSheet.Range("A1").AutoFilter
End If
End Sub


'Turn off AutoFilter with VBA:
Sub TurnFilterOff()
Worksheets("Sheet1").AutoFilterMode = False
End Sub
```

Tip 67: Highlight duplicate rows macro

As discussed before, Excel has a tool to remove duplicate entries, and you can highlight duplicate cells. But what if you want to highlight duplicate rows?

```
Sub DupsinRed()
 Application.ScreenUpdating = False
Rng = Selection.Rows.Count
For i = Rng To 1 Step -1
myCheck = ActiveCell
ActiveCell.Offset(1, 0).Select
 For j = 1 To i
 If ActiveCell = myCheck Then
 Selection.Font.Bold = True
 Selection.Font.ColorIndex = 3
```

```
End If
ActiveCell.Offset(1, 0).Select
Next j
ActiveCell.Offset(-i, 0).Select
Next i
Application.ScreenUpdating = True
End Sub
```

The statement "Application.ScreenUpdating = False" prevents the screen from updating to ensure the macro runs faster and the screen will not flicker. Don't forget to set it back to "True".

Tip 68: Create folders from Excel

I often find myself having to create multiple folders and directories before beginning a new project. Many others may take the time consuming method of doing this by hand but you can actually save yourself a lot of time by using a simple VBA macro in an Excel spreadsheet. One method of doing this is to start a new spreadsheet and save it as a macro-enabled workbook in the location where you want to create the multiple folders (such as C:\Work Directory\Parts List).

Next, in column A list all the names of the folders you want to create. Now, hold the "Alt" key down and press "F8" to open the Macros window. Enter the name "CreateFolders" and click the Create button which will open the macro editor. You can copy and paste the following code:

```
Sub Create_Folders()
OpenAt = "My computer:\ "
Set ShellApp =
CreateObject("Shell.Application").BrowseForFolder(0, "Please
Choose The Folder For This Project", 0, OpenAt)
```

```
'Set the folder to that selected. (On error in case cancelled)
On Error Resume Next
BrowseForFolder = ShellApp.Self.Path

'create the folders where-ever the workbook is saved
Dim Rng As Range
Dim maxRows, maxCols, r, c As Integer
Set Rng = Selection
maxRows = Rng.Rows.Count
maxCols = Rng.Columns.Count

For c = 1 To maxCols
r = 1
Do While r <= maxRows
If  Len(Dir(ActiveWorkbook.Path  &  "\"  &  Rng(r,  c),
vbDirectory)) = 0 Then
MkDir (BrowseForFolder & "\" & Rng(r, c))

On Error Resume Next
End If
r = r + 1
Loop

Next c
End Sub
```

Now all you have to do is highlight the cells and run the macro. Your folders are automatically created just like that! Save the macro and you can use it over and over again, saving you lots of time and impressing your fellow employees!

Tips 69: Combine workbooks

If you have multiple spreadsheets you can use a macro to automatically combine them into one workbook.

```
Option Explicit

'32-bit API declarations
Declare Function SHGetPathFromIDList Lib "shell32.dll" _
Alias "SHGetPathFromIDListA" (ByVal pidl As Long,
ByVal pszpath As String) As Long

Declare Function SHBrowseForFolder Lib "shell32.dll" _
Alias "SHBrowseForFolderA" (lpBrowseInfo As
BrowseInfo) As Long

Public Type BrowseInfo
    hOwner As Long
    pIDLRoot As Long
    pszDisplayName As String
    lpszTitle As String
    ulFlags As Long
    lpfn As Long
    lParam As Long
    iImage As Long
End Type

Function GetDirectory(Optional msg) As String
    On Error Resume Next
    Dim bInfo As BrowseInfo
    Dim path As String
    Dim r As Long, x As Long, pos As Integer

    'Root folder = Desktop
    bInfo.pIDLRoot = 0&
```

```
        'Title in the dialog
     If IsMissing(msg) Then
     bInfo.lpszTitle = "Please select the folder of the excel files to
copy."
        Else
           bInfo.lpszTitle = msg
        End If

        'Type of directory to return
        bInfo.ulFlags = &H1

        'Display the dialog
        x = SHBrowseForFolder(bInfo)

        'Parse the result
        path = Space$(512)
        r = SHGetPathFromIDList(ByVal x, ByVal path)
        If r Then
           pos = InStr(path, Chr$(0))
           GetDirectory = Left(path, pos - 1)
        Else
           GetDirectory = ""
        End If
     End Function

     Sub Combine_Workbooks()
        Dim path        As String
        Dim FileName        As String
        Dim LastCell        As Range
        Dim Wkb        As Workbook
        Dim WS        As Worksheet
        Dim ThisWB        As String

        ThisWB = ThisWorkbook.Name
        Application.EnableEvents = False
        Application.ScreenUpdating = False
        path = GetDirectory
```

```
FileName = Dir(path & " \ *.xls", vbNormal)
Do Until FileName = " "
    If FileName <> ThisWB Then
Set Wkb = Workbooks.Open(FileName:=path & " \ " &
FileName)

For Each WS In Wkb.Worksheets
Set LastCell = WS.Cells.SpecialCells(xlCellTypeLastCell)

If  LastCell.Value  =  " "  And  LastCell.Address  =
Range("$A$1").Address Then
            Else
                WS.Copy
After:=ThisWorkbook.Sheets(ThisWorkbook.Sheets.Count)
            End If
        Next WS
        Wkb.Close False
    End If
    FileName = Dir()
Loop
Application.EnableEvents = True

Set Wkb = Nothing
Set LastCell = Nothing
'========================

'delete the original sheet
Application.DisplayAlerts = False
Sheets("Combine_Workbooks Master").Select
ActiveWindow.SelectedSheets.Delete
Sheets("Resources").Select
ActiveWindow.SelectedSheets.Delete
Sheets("Info").Select
ActiveWindow.SelectedSheets.Delete
Application.DisplayAlerts = True
```

```
    Dim fileSaveName As String
    Dim CurrentFile As String
    Dim NewFile As String
    Dim NewFileType As String
    Dim NewFileName As String

    CurrentFile = ThisWorkbook.FullName

    NewFileType = "Excel Files 1997-2003 (*.xls), *.xls," &
"Excel Files 2007 (*.xlsx), *.xlsx," & "All files (*.*), *.*"

    NewFile                                              =
Application.GetSaveAsFilename(InitialFileName:=NewFileName,
fileFilter:=NewFileType)
        If NewFile <> "" And NewFile <> "False" Then
            ActiveWorkbook.SaveAs FileName:=NewFile, _
                FileFormat:=xlNormal, _
                Password:="", _
                WriteResPassword:="", _
                ReadOnlyRecommended:=False, _
                CreateBackup:=False

            Else
        MsgBox     "Changes     not     saved!",     vbExclamation,
Title:=NewFileName & ".xls"

        End If
         Application.ScreenUpdating = True
        End Sub
```

Watch a video of this process in action:

https://www.youtube.com/watch?v=fnpT0vIZUpw&feature=player_embedded

Tip 70: Export to Word, PPT, etc.

The first thing we need to do is create a new instance of Microsoft Word and make it visible:

```
Dim appWD As Word.Application
Set appWD = CreateObject("Word.Application")
appWD.Visible = True
```

Next, let's find the last row that contains data within our active Excel spreadsheet (my sheet is called "Data"):

```
Sheets("Data").Select
Dim FinalRow As Integer
FinalRow = Range("A9999").End(xlUp).Row
```

Now we add some error handling - if there is no data then quit the program, otherwise continue on:

```
If FinalRow = 0 Then
        Exit Sub
        Else
```

As a check, I like to have a message box pop-up displaying the total number of rows with data:

```
MsgBox "Number of rows is " & FinalRow
```

Now it's time to tell Word to create a new document. We'll also add our header text by using TypeText. TypeParagraph inserts a new paragraph by going to the next line:

```
appWD.Documents.Add
appWD.Selection.TypeParagraph
appWD.Selection.TypeText Text:="[table caption= List of
Data]"
appWD.Selection.TypeParagraph
appWD.Selection.TypeText Text:="Name,Height(m)"
```

Next, we'll create a For...Next loop to cycle through every row and look to see if there is a hyperlink in column A. If there is a hyperlink, we want to copy it, if not then we still want to copy any text in the cell.

```
Dim hyperlink1 As String
Dim i As Integer
For i = 2 To FinalRow
If Range("A" & i).Hyperlinks.Count > 0 Then
'if there is a hyperlink
```

```
appWD.Selection.TypeParagraph
hyperlink1 = Range("A" & i).Hyperlinks(1).Address

appWD.ActiveDocument.Hyperlinks.Add
Anchor:=appWD.Selection.Range,    Address:=hyperlink1,
SubAddress:="", ScreenTip:="", TextToDisplay:=Range("A" & i)


appWD.Selection.TypeText Text:="," & Range("B" & i)

Else
'If no hyperlink

appWD.Selection.TypeParagraph
appWD.Selection.TypeText   Text:=Range("A"  &  i)  &  ","  &
Range("B" & i)

End If
Next 'i
```

Finally, we can add any text at the bottom of the document and close the if and sub statements.

```
'end the table
appWD.Selection.TypeParagraph
appWD.Selection.TypeText Text:="[/table]"
End If
End Sub
```

Tip 71: Protect your macros

To protect your code, open the Excel Workbook and go to **Tools>Macro>Visual Basic Editor (Alt+F11)**. Now, from within the VBE go to **Tools>VBAProject Properties** and then click the Protection page tab and then check "Lock project from viewing" and then enter your password and again to confirm it. After doing this you must save, close & reopen the Workbook for the protection to take effect.

Tip 72: How to Decrease Your Productivity

If you want to have some fun with your coworkers, here are some tips to DECREASE your productivity, through pranks and practical jokes:
http://excelspreadsheetshelp.blogspot.com/2013/06/exc el-pranks-and-practical-jokes-with.html
For example: Have a message box pop-up asking if the user wants to download the virus they requested. Whether they press the yes or no button the next message tells them the virus has begun downloading!

Private Sub Workbook_Open()

MsgBox "The virus you requested is now ready to download, Do you want to start downloading now?", vbYesNo, "Virus Trojan-x45fju"
MsgBox "The Virus is Now Downloading. You have made the biggest mistake of your life! ByE bYe", , "Begin Virus Download"
End Sub

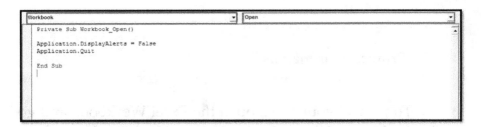

Chapter 7: What to do when you get stuck

You're trying to write an Excel formula or macro but now you're simply stuck and don't know what to do next. Or maybe it's just not working the way you intended it to. How in the world are you supposed to go on from this point? If you're new to Microsoft Excel you're likely going to be dead in the water until you get some help. Before giving up, there are a few steps I recommend you take to try and figure the solution out for yourself. I strongly believe you learn more through struggling, overcoming obstacles, and doing it yourself. Here is my list of actions you should take if you consider yourself stuck:

Tip 73: Common Excel formula mistakes

If a formula is not working as expected check for these common mistakes, as the cause is most likely human error in entering the formula:

- Spelling (function names are correct)
- All parentheses are closed (they are colored coded to help you)
- Commas where needed
- Quotations where needed
- No circular references (references the cell where the formula is located)

If these are all correct and the formula is still not working as you expect it then maybe you are using the wrong function? Chances are though, that you just entered something incorrectly or missed something as seemingly insignificant as a comma.

Tip 74: Use Previous Examples

A great way to learn is by dissecting templates to see how other users solved similar problems. Remember to check for things like named ranges and conditional formatting. I've made a number of my Excel spreadsheets **available as a free download**. I often send sample macros in my email newsletter as well. Also, be sure to read all of my blog posts as many of them have custom code with thorough explanations of how they work. Forums such as Mr Excel are also a great place to see macro examples. Posting in the recommend forums listed in the resources at the end of this book is a great way to get feedback from multiple power users.

Tip 75: Step Away From the Problem

This is actually my favorite tip in this section. There have been countless times where I've been banging my head against a wall, not able to figure out a problem. So, I would simply get up from my computer and walk away, maybe for a few hours or days, and not think about the problem at all. Then when I sit down in front of the screen again refreshed the answer hits me almost immediately. Seriously, this happens almost every time! It's that whole not being able to see the forest through the trees type of thing. So take a break!

Tip 76: Use the Internet to Ask Questions

Google is your friend! If you don't find a suitable answer on your first search try a new one with different words. Personally, there's nothing that annoys me more than when someone asks me a question and I simply Google it and I find the solution right away. Don't be lazy! Other people do not want to do your work for you.

Chapter 8: The Final Word

Excel is a software Swiss army knife, from number crunching to creating charts, organizing lists to automating complex tasks, Excel can do it all. Some unique uses of Excel spreadsheets you may not have thought of before:

> ➤ A role playing video game created with macros
> ➤ A 3D graphics engine
> ➤ Weight loss tracker
> ➤ Digital flash cards for studying
> ➤ Recreate board games like Monopoly
> ➤ Build mockups of your house, website, or other project
> ➤ Seating chart for wedding dinner
> ➤ Outline an ebook
> ➤ Graphic design and other artwork
> ➤ Scrabble scoring system
> ➤ Wine inventory
> ➤ Database website creation
> ➤ Play Pac Man
> ➤ Design a roller coaster
> ➤ Scoring for a horseshoe or other sports league
> ➤ Compare multiple apartments or other products
> ➤ Create a checklist
> ➤ Pilot training

Even though you might spend most of your time using Excel to make lists, crunch numbers, and accomplish general tasks, that doesn't mean that there aren't other interesting uses for this incredible program. It takes an experienced user to do so, and the more familiar you are with all of Excel's features, the more quickly your tasks can be accomplished. There are multiple ways to do things in Excel but one of those ways is probably better than the others, you just have to figure out which method that is. Saving a little bit of time here and there can add up over a long period of time, such as your professional career. Try out some of these tips and take your Excel skills to the next level!

I hope this guide has helped you find a better way to do a few of your tasks and accomplish your goals. Thank you for reading and here's to your success!

-Nick Weisenberger
http://excelspreadsheetshelp.blogspot.com

P.S. I hope you enjoyed reading. Please consider returning to your point of purchase and leave an honest review!

Appendix I: Symbol Shortcuts

The following is a list of shortcuts to generate symbols:

Alt + 0176 = ° (Degrees)
Alt + 0149 = • (Bullet)
Alt + 0162 = ¢
Alt + 0188 = ¼
Alt + 0189 = ½
Alt + 0190 = ¾
Alt + 0177 = ±
Alt + 0178 = ²
Alt + 0179 = ³
Alt + 0163 = £
Alt + 0128 = €
Alt + 0151 = — (m dash)
Alt + 0150 = - (n dash)
Alt + 0187 = »
Alt + 0169 = ©
Alt + 0174 = ®
Alt + 0165 = ¥
Alt + 0177 = ±
Alt + 0247 = ÷
Alt + 0166 = ¦
Alt + 0134 = †
Alt + 0227 = ã
Alt + 0191 = ¿
Alt + 0161 = ¡
Alt + 0209 = Ñ
Alt + 0241 = ñ
Alt + 0225 = á
Alt + 0233 = é
Alt + 0237 = í
Alt + 0243 = ó
Alt + 0250 = ú
Alt + 0252 = ü
Alt + 0186 = ° (1° = primero)
Alt + 0170 = ² (2² = segunda)

Appendix II: Shortcuts Quick Reference

20 Useful Excel Shortcuts
http://excelspreadsheetshelp.blogspot.com

1. F1: Access the Excel help file
2. Ctrl+`: Show or hide formulas
3. Alt: Access the ribbon
4. Ctrl+; Enter the current date
5. Ctrl+PgUp/PgDn: Navigate between worksheets
6. Ctrl/Shift+Space: Select an entire row or column
7. Alt+ =: Sum function
8. CRTL+ UP/DOWN: Jump to top or bottom
9. Alt+Enter: Multiple lines in one cell (line break)
10. CRTL+0/9: Hide columns or rows
11. F6: Switch between tools
12. CRTL + ': Copy cell above selected
13. ESC: Cancel changes
14. Shift + F3 : List of functions
15. Crtl+g; Create bookmarks and select all comments
16. CRTL+1: Format cells
17. F4: Toggle a reference
18. CRTL+ALT+SHIFT+F9: Update formulas
19. CTRL+SHIFT+~: Change date to number format
20. Alt + F11: Open macro editor

Appendix III: Tools and Resources

I thought it would be helpful to create a resource page that you can always come to for all of your Excel spreadsheet needs.

Where to Get Your Excel Questions Answered

Mr. Excel Forum: The place to go to get your Excel questions answered by Excel gurus and experts. Other users have probably asked the same questions as you have.
http://www.mrexcel.com/forum/forum.php

Eng Tips Forum: If you have an Excel question related to the field of engineering you can post your question in this excellent forum.
http://www.eng-tips.com/threadminder.cfm?pid=770

Stackoverflow: Use this site to ask questions when you get stuck with your macros and there are tons of knowledgeable programmers willing to help you out.
http://stackoverflow.com/

Contact Me: I'll do my best to respond to you in a timely matter but due to the number of emails I get daily it may take some time, please be patient:
http://excelspreadsheetshelp.blogspot.com

Online Excel Viewers

Bonus Tip: Avoid vertically oriented text in your spreadsheets as vertical text is sometimes not compatible with Google Docs or Excel Web App.

Office Online Web App - Save documents, spreadsheets, and presentations online, in OneDrive. Share them with others and work together at the same time. Get started now, it's free!
https://office.com/start/default.aspx

Google Docs - Easily upload all kinds of docs and share them with others. Documents can be edited by multiple users simultaneously.
http://drive.google.com/

Zoho Excel Viewer - Easy to use online viewer
https://sheet.zoho.com/excelviewer

EditGrid Viewer - Another online viewer option
http://www.editgrid.com/viewer

View Docs Online - Supports all the popular Microsoft platforms including Excel
http://www.viewdocsonline.com/

Tools to Increase Your Excel Knowledge and Skills

There are several methods to help improve your Excel proficiency including books, websites, and training classes. Below are the ones I recommend and have experience with.

Excel Books

Microsoft Excel 2013 In Depth by Bill Jelen: Known as Mr. Excel, Bill Jelen is a Microsoft Excel MVP. This book literally covers everything you'd want to know about Excel 2013.

101 Secrets of a Microsoft Excel Addict: Discover little-known Excel secrets that have been hiding right under your nose that will help boost your Excel skills and productivity far ahead of everyone around you.

Excel 2010 Bible by John Walkenbach: This is by far the best Excel book I have ever found for anyone who uses Microsoft Excel spreadsheets on a daily basis.

Excel VBA Macro Programming Links

Error Trapping with Visual Basic for Applications: Complete list of error codes when using the Err function.
http://support.microsoft.com/kb/146864

Microsoft Excel Object Model: Microsoft's MSDN online library is the best place for finding out information about the Microsoft Office object model for VBA.
http://msdn.microsoft.com/en-us/library/wss56bz7%28v=vs.80%29.aspx

Microsoft Visual Basic 2010 Step by Step by Michael Halvorson: A lot of hands-on work-by-examples will further the development of your Visual Basic programming skills.

VBScript Functions: A comprehensive list and description of VBScript functions you can use in your Excel macros.
http://www.w3schools.com/vbscript/vbscript_ref_functions.asp

Miscellaneous Excel Resources

11 Best YouTube Channels to Learn Excel: There are some great Excel tutorials on YouTube. Don't waste time sorting through all the bad ones; I've listed the best channels here. http://excelspreadsheetshelp.blogspot.com/2014/03/11-best-excel-video-tutorial-channels.html

Project management spreadsheet templates: I've created and used numerous Excel spreadsheets on various projects over the years. Recently, I assembled all of my most useful spreadsheets into one giant master file that you can download for free (after joining my email list). http://excelspreadsheetshelp.blogspot.com/p/project-management.html

Microsoft Surface 2: Hands down the best tablet for Excel and other Microsoft Office products. In fact, it comes with fully functional versions of Excel, Word, Outlook, PowerPoint, and OneNote for free.

Simple Spreadsheet: A free simple spreadsheet Android application.